PRAISE FOR
Soul Self

You might call Jack Stephens book *Soul Self* a self-help book. And it is that. A good one, with a Spirit and permaculture inspired set of basic exercises that can help you reorganize the garden of your personality around an organic relationship to your own Soul. For some, this might be called your "higher self," or "deeper self," I guess. In Richard Schwartz's book, *Internal Family Systems Therapy*, it's called the "Self" (upper case "S") or "Center"—as distinguished from various confused subpersonalities. Whatever we call it, it's the part of you that conveys clear, connected guidance about how best to live a rich and fulfilling life.

You'll notice I've said the exercises "can help you." This is a book to DO, not just skim through. On the surface, some of what's recommended looks too simple. It's not until you pause, take the deeper breaths, and enact an exercise or two—that you start to get the message. It works if you work it, and when you do, it really IS simple. To help engage you in that essential pause, those moments of becoming present—Jack has some wonderful wisdom stories and analogies. Some are going to engage with deeper issues as they do this, and for them there may be more techniques that can help. But I believe Jack is covering those in a sequel or two.

Despite all this good stuff, *Soul Self* is not just a self-help book. In the background, woven through the pages, it's also an unabashed, flat-out love story. Jack was an organized, outwardly focused, not-very-present guy until his life and awareness were turned upside down by a great love. It's one that continues now in the form of his psychically gifted partner, Stacey, and the work they do together to help others on the path. What if, guided by your own Soul, your path can be just as rich?

~ MICHAEL REDDY, PhD, author of *Health, Happiness, & Family Constellations*

"*Soul Self* is an outstanding primer on living a Soul-directed life. It should be required reading for every student in high school and college. If I had been given this book at that age, I would have saved decades of searching, seeking, and experimenting to find my own Soul path. Jack Stephens has taken one of Life's Big Questions – "How shall I live?" – and offered a step-by-step manual for finding the answer. His key? Quiet the mind and listen to your Soul's guidance. Establish a direct dialogue with the most objective and spiritual part of yourself. You can't go wrong. When your Soul is in charge of your life, rather than your ego, you can achieve what you really want. This book is a great beginning for your quest for a better life."

~ LION GOODMAN, author of *Transform Your Beliefs: Unleash Your Magnificence & Change Your World*

"This is a wonderful book that guides you to look at yourself from a deeper, Spirit-inspired place. When you read this book you will recognize your still small voice that has been calling you, and understand the tools to communicate more clearly with your Soul. Jack Stephens does a wonderful job of giving you the tools to communicate with your Soul. He teaches you, in a very concrete way, how to discern the voice of your own inner wisdom and compassion. The answers are within you – within your very Soul. You will not be disappointed with this book and guide."

~ VERONIKA TRACY-SMITH, PhD, author of *Meditation Now: Your Guide to Building a Simple Practice*

"Whether you are a new Seeker or a seasoned traveler on the journey to self-discovery, *Soul Self* is a book that you must read. Having read numerous books in the same genre, I found this one to be both clear and simplistic in its message. A wonderful, inspiring book! Well Done!"

~ SAMANTHA HERRON, spiritual counselor and minister

"Jack Stephens shows compassion for all those who have dared, or are daring, to even consider making the life changing decision about living from their Soul / Heart. He gently and honestly presents a succession of what I call "baby steps", and includes encouraging explanations and short, valuable exercises. His metaphors and one fable attach to the mind comfortably, begging to be tools along one's path. For me, this is a book I'll revisit often, knowing that each reread will spark an 'ah-ha' and a sense of 'at-a-girl' as I continue on this joyous path with Soul in charge. I encourage you to buy this book and then share a copy with others."

~ CARRIE LOUISE, author of *Soul Being Soul*

"I read *Soul Self* cover to cover in one sitting, which is no small accomplishment and a compliment to the author. Jack Stephens' *Soul Self* engaged me with wisdom I found throughout the pages. He starts off with a wonderful and instructional analogy about a horse and its rider (as it relates to your personal journey through life). Then a few pages later you get to *'Pebbles: A Fable.'* This simple, powerful story is worth the price of admission alone. The wisdom in just these three pages will do wonders for your spiritual journey if practiced! *Soul Self* contains very important lessons and simple yet essential practices on 'what to do' when you experience conflict between the ego-mind and your real Self. I agree that we all have a self-chosen reason for being here on this planet at this time. I know firsthand of the importance of getting in touch with your Soul or Self. If you're looking for guidance about your Soul's Blueprint, or just need a reminder, you'll find helpful, confirming, and inspiring answers in *Soul Self*. Jack, thanks for getting your message out to a world in need of such a message."

~ KEN OBERMEYER, author of *The Journey to Joy: Reconnecting with the Real You*

Soul Self

How to Tame Your Mind, Uncover Your Blueprint, & Live Your Soul Purpose

Jack Stephens

For my beloved wife, Stacey:
With Infinite Gratitude

Soul Self Living Publications
Reno, Nevada

SOUL SELF

Copyright © Jack Stephens, 2012

All Rights Reserved. No part of this book may be reproduced in any form, by photocopying or by any electronic, photographic or mechanical means, or in the form of a phonographic recording; nor may it be stored in a retrieval system, transmitted, or otherwise be copied for public or private use – other than for "fair use" as brief quotations embodied in articles and reviews - without prior permission in writing from both the copyright owner and the publisher.

The author of this book does not dispense medical advice or prescribe the use of any technique as a form of treatment for physical, emotional, or medical problems without the advice of a physician, either directly or indirectly. The intent of the author is only to offer information of a general nature to help you in your quest for emotional and spiritual well-being. In the event you use any of the information in this book for yourself, which is your constitutional right, the author and the publisher assume no responsibility for your actions.

First Published 2012 by
Soul Self Living Publications
(a division of Soul Self Living, Inc.) www.SoulSelfLiving.com
Edited by Stacey Stephens

ISBN: 0615919332
ISBN-13: 978-0-615-91933-1
SoulSelfLiving.com

Acknowledgments

First and foremost, I am most grateful for my beloved Soulmate Stacey. From the moment we met she dedicated herself to help me Awaken my Soul. Her wisdom, energy, compassion and patience inspired me to apply her teachings to experience my Soul Self. It is my profound privilege to introduce you to her through this book.

I am also deeply grateful to The Ancient Ones for assisting me along my journey to an ever greater life of love, joy and fulfillment.

Contents

Preface	xv

Part I: Distinguishing Between the Ego and Soul

Are You the Rider, Or the Horse?	1
Soul Authority	4
A Successful Voyage	6
Locating the Ego-mind	7
The Soul Center	9
Heart-Centered Decisions	10
Real Love	11
The Library of the Mind	11
Soul Freedom	13
Our Feelings Are Indicators	14
Upgrading Your Library	15
Staying in the Saddle	17
Apply the Wisdom	18
Pebbles: A Fable	19
From The Ancient Ones: The Human Make-Up	22

Part II: Finding Your True Voice

The Soul's Knowing	24
Life-Force Energy	24
The Pond of Perception	26
Cultivating a Relationship with Your Self	27
Why Wait?	28
Positive Interpretation	30
Raising Consciousness	31
Forgiveness	33
The Process of Forgiveness	34
Uncovering Your Blueprint	36
Fulfilling Your Mission	37
Key Questions for Uncovering Your Blueprint	38
Savor Your Soul	39
Apply the Wisdom	41
From The Ancient Ones: Inner Authority	42

Part III: Being Your Self: Acting on Your Soul's Direction

Your Divine Nature	44
Decide, Align, Act	45
Soul-Centered Decision Making	46
Even the Hard Way Will Get You There…Eventually	47
The Garden of Your Life	49
Utilize Ancient Wisdom Today	51
Conscious Evolution	52
Breaking the Chains of Victimhood	52
The Pendulum Swing	54
Inner Balance	55
Know When to Ask for Help	56
Apply the Wisdom	57
From The Ancient Ones: Action	58
Afterword	59

Preface

Soul Self emerged directly from an unexpected five-month retreat on the Island of Hawai'i and the profound Soul Awakening I experienced during that time. I had anticipated a few weeks of writing, swimming, lounging on the beach and sipping mai tais under a coconut tree. Instead, I sat in silent meditation and ego- mind renovation assisted by a remarkable Healer and gifted spiritual teacher.

I met Stacey at the home of our mutual friend, Jim Channon. Prior to introducing us, Jim described her to me as the most complete healer and accurate psychic he had met through several decades of engaging with renowned spiritual teachers and mystics in his world travels. I felt electrified by the opportunity to meet her personally, and thrilled when she agreed to spend a few hours with me.

That meeting would change the course of both of our lives. She would become my friend, guru, constant companion and, eventually, my wife. We were Soulmates finally reuniting.

The Ego Struggle

Just a year earlier, I had left a career as a sustainability and business consultant to become a spiritual coach. I had spent many years reading, attending seminars, and studying with various teachers. I had gained skills to assist others and my practice was growing. I enjoyed helping people by using my training. However, few of my clients were experiencing lasting benefit. I was not helping them truly change the root beliefs underlying their issues.

There was also an obvious disconnection between my library of knowledge and my personal experience. I could convincingly talk about positive, healthy living, but I could not yet match those words with my actions. I was depressed and often ill. I struggled to "fake it until making it." I had tried many types of energetic and psychological techniques, talk therapy and affirmations to change my unfulfilled life. However, nothing I did went deep enough, so the changes I made were mostly superficial.

Although I experienced various successes in my life, they never seemed to last or bring a true sense of fulfillment. Like many people in modern society, I spent most of my life doing what I learned as a child – striving to please others, looking outside of my Self for direction and competing for recognition, affection and seemingly scarce resources. I let subconscious programs, unhealed trauma, and opinions of other people control my life. I learned about the power of positive thinking, but I mistakenly believed that a few minutes of constructive thought every now and then would overwrite the deeply buried, firmly ignored or resolutely avoided destructive thoughts, feelings and beliefs that were creating my reality 95% of the time.

Knowing that we all want to be happy, yet continuing to make choices that cause unhappiness is all too common. However, I felt alone in my feelings of confusion, self-criticism and despair. I had a difficult time accepting that I was worthy or capable of experiencing health, prosperity and true, loving partnership. I did my best to disguise my insecurities, and over time, I accepted that while I was neither a dismal failure nor a grand success, the life I was living was the best I could expect. In nearly every area of my life, I settled for less than I was capable of creating. Fortunately, one wise decision can overwrite a myriad of foolish ones.

Soul Awakening

Meeting Stacey changed everything for me. As a desert traveler celebrates their arrival at an oasis, I rejuvenated in her presence. During our first conversation I felt lighter, then happier, then joyful! I was quenching my thirst for true connection as she showed me the Source of life-force energy that was deep within me. She helped me awaken my Soul.

This burst of immense joy gave me brilliant flashes of insight about my life. I clearly saw the jagged path I had taken through the first forty years of my life. I knew that if I continued living as I had been I would never experience genuine fulfillment in my life. I also saw a much brighter future full of possibilities. I thoroughly comprehended that I would have to make significant changes if I wanted to bring them about. After only a few sessions with Stacey, I found the courage to do just that.

I decided to do whatever was required to expand my Soul awakening experience. I cancelled my ticket home, ended (yet another) unfulfilling long-term relationship and focused on recreating my life from the ground up. The decision to make a real change was easy; the repercussions were a challenge to navigate. Few friends or family members supported my decision. Many condemned me. I surrendered all of my possessions, assets and most of my clients and friends. As many seekers of every culture and spiritual tradition had done before me, I became an acolyte at the feet of a master. I entered the cave of wisdom for a retreat from the world that would last more than two years.

From Ego-Driven to Soul-Guided

My teacher was unlike anyone I had ever met. She had navigated a life path of extreme difficulty and faced nearly every challenge a woman can. Through it all she maintained an otherworldly grace, and used her experiences as parables to assist others. Her presence and wisdom awakens people to their divinity, heals their maladies, and renews their enthusiasm for life. She has been called an American guru, and I had her nearly undivided attention.

Stacey shared with me her own wisdom as well as that of the non-physical Beings who call themselves, "The Ancient Ones". Stacey is a channel for The Ancient Ones, and they regularly communicate through her. We are grateful for their close friendship, and for sharing the vital wisdom they have for us at this time in our planetary conscious evolution.

I have not always been open to such unconventional guidance, but when confronted with spiritual truth that laid bare the illusions of my ego, I could not deny either the wisdom or the source. Stacey and The Ancient Ones held a mirror for me to see the divinity we all have within, and I am grateful for their assistance. This book can be a mirror for you, to discover and express your inner brilliance and Soul purpose.

In these pages, you will read what is a melding of perspectives: Stacey's, mine and The Ancient Ones. Core wisdom from Stacey's years as a Healer and spiritual teacher provides the bones of this book. I give flesh to the bones by providing insights, from my own life, of how this wisdom can be applied in yours. The Ancient Ones provide timeless perspective of the human potential through clear guidance received by Stacey. This work has been a team effort, and while the insights I share are from my journey, I share full credit with my collaborators.

My process of writing has been a journey of generous coaching from Stacey, listening to the teachings of The Ancient Ones, drawing from the knowledge of my life experience, then discovering the lessons and expressing the wisdom that has emerged as I have applied myself to the new understandings. I have personally tested the material in this book and found it to be more effective in assisting me to live my life with purpose than any other training, teaching or educational experience I have had previously.

As a result of this work, I discovered inner knowing that had been yearning to break free for a lifetime. I uncovered precious keys to unlock the prison cell created by my limited ego-mind, and release my Soul that it had unwittingly held captive. Utilizing these keys, I experienced the awakening of my body, mind and Soul's expression.

I joyfully share these keys with you in Soul Self, so that you may liberate your brilliance and beauty, and allow divine intelligence, life-force energy, and unlimited power of Spirit to flow through you and express AS YOU!

Soul Self

In this book, I teach a process of aligning and balancing the Soul, ego-mind and body to become the Soul Self. This requires focused attention and commitment. It results in profound reorganization from an ego-driven life into a Soul-guided one, which I am calling *Soul Self Living*. Every person is capable of uncovering their intrinsic inner knowing, visioning and creating ability that is far beyond what most of us have imagined. When you apply the knowledge and wisdom contained in these pages, you can reveal your powerful inner guidance, and enjoy a life of wonder and fulfillment! It is my hope that the information in this book will assist you in awakening into your Soul Self life.

We are all unique expressions of divine energy that unites all of existence. We are brothers and sisters who have chosen to embody now for a collective celebration of our lives as conscious co-creators. By utilizing our inner divine guidance, we all have the means to enjoy lives of insight and inspiration, and we are all capable of much more than we have yet expressed.

It is with immense joy that I share with you the wisdom and teachings of The Ancient Ones. It is my hope that this book will inspire you to have your own direct experience of your Soul Self, which you can then share with others, igniting a chain reaction that can exponentially change the world from the inside out. This is a book, not of *the truth*, but of *my truth*, and a resource intended to support you in finding *your truth*.

Operating Instructions

The words in *Soul Self* have layers of meaning and energy so that you can be vibrationally tuned to the truth of your own Soul, which you can feel and experience. This knowing will unfold and reveal itself to you as you gain deeper levels of understanding over time. Because our backgrounds differ, our personal definition of the words may not always match. That is why it is useful to maintain an open heart and mind while you read.

Utilize the exercises in this book on a regular basis to support the reshaping of your perceptions and elimination of negative patterns, thoughts and programs. You may gain new insights with each reading of the material, as you are able to uncover deeper awareness to assist in your unfoldment. Accept personal ownership of your truths, insights and understandings as they reveal themselves to you through your study.

Take your time as you read, and allow your body and mind to relax. Permit yourself to feel when a phrase or sentence has an inner effect. Pause to allow the process to unfold, and let the inner shift become a conscious expansion into higher awareness and greater understanding. You are on a journey of Self-mastery, and practice makes the master.

Soul Self Living

To emphasize the contrast between the ego-driven life and the Soul-guided life, I share with you clear, practical, and proven ways to benefit from the lessons inside your mistakes. We all know the negative results of making choices from trauma, training and programming. Most of us have made the majority of our mistakes in ignorance because the ego-programs that drive our decisions are mainly invisible to us. However, once we are aware of them we can take full responsibility, and then make wiser choices.

Today, I am living a Soul-guided life of true joy, and I am so pleased by the changes I have made. While they have not been without challenges, the results are deeply satisfying. I am enjoying clearer intuition, stronger instincts and the positive results of following my inner wisdom. Every key relationship in my life has improved, especially the one with my Self. Doors are opening, and opportunities are unfolding with surprising speed.

We are able to design our lives to be journeys of positive, joyful and abundant creation, because we are born with divine capabilities. Fulfilling this birthright is the purpose of Soul Self Living. We need only bring our Soul, ego-mind, and body into aligned balance, for our inner guidance to function properly. Use this as a guidebook to unveil and utilize yours.

We have the potential to become living examples of true human beings, free to live as divine co-creators. As we listen within, accept our divinity, express our true nature and cultivate positive relationships we can contribute to humanity's shift into higher-consciousness living.

As you apply the wisdom contained in this book may you love your life as I now love mine! May you connect to the passion of your purpose, and experience vitality, joy and fulfillment as your Soul Self.

1

Distinguishing Between the Ego and Soul

You are here on this abundant planet, in this exceptional era, with your intelligence, physicality, and talents, to enjoy a life that can only be expressed by YOU. You are worthy and capable of creating a life of joy and fulfillment. You are a unique expression of Universal Spirit, and the world needs your full participation.

Are you willing to remove the obstacles, limitations, fears, negative programs and beliefs that dim your divine light? Do you want to truly enjoy your life and share your gifts with others? Then decide…

Are You the Rider, Or the Horse?

It is your divinity, your intuition, your inner wisdom, your insights, your visions, these mystical parts of you that are designed to guide you. You are capable of hearing your inner voice, knowing your purpose and being aware of the next step at any given moment. Your internal guidance is already working within you. However, most of us have never received operating instructions. Instead, nearly all of us have directed our lives with our ego-minds.

Imagine that your body, ego-mind and Soul are like a horse and rider. Picture your body as the horse, your ego-mind as the horse's mind, and your Soul as the rider. Before you embodied, the rider had made preparations for your life's journey. Your Soul planned an incredible ride, full of adventure, challenge and enjoyment. After your birth, however, society, your parents, family, friends, teachers and religion primarily saw a horse that needed to be trained. Most of them were unaware that you came with your own inner guidance, your own rider. They may have acknowledged that you had a Soul with a purpose, but often with the best intentions, it was the horse — your body and your ego- mind — that got the attention.

If you have ever ridden a horse, you may have felt a little intimidated the first time you got on its back. As a child growing up in a rural area where it was common to own horses, I felt amazed at the immense size and power of these animals. Like most new riders, I learned that a horse is not only big and strong, but it has a mind of its own. It will go where *it* wants to unless it surrenders command to *the rider*.

An experienced rider knows in advance what he or she wants from the horse and conveys it to the animal with clear intention. The rider gives the horse a purpose for the ride, tasks to accomplish along the way, and sees to its needs. The rider provides direction, and the horse takes action.

Both the horse and rider can enjoy the journey together when the horse properly surrenders to its master. This powerful animal goes where directed, because it accepts the rider's leadership, competence, and care. They become a team in perfect harmony with each other. When a horse and rider work in unison, they can quickly travel long distances, and they can accomplish remarkable things together.

Unfortunately, the ego-mind grows strong and powerful with all of the focused training it gets. It becomes convinced that it is in charge, and makes decisions based upon what it thinks and believes. However, most of your beliefs have been subconsciously accepted from someone else! Your mind is molded, programmed and controlled by others, beginning in the womb.[i] You build your daily thoughts and behaviors upon the foundation of these inherited or unconsciously accepted beliefs or programs. These false programs are running your decision-making process and, if you are like most people, you have accepted them over your Soul's real plans. This puts the *rider* at the mercy of the *horse*. The ego goes where *it* wants to, and you wonder how you end up in experiences your Soul had *no intention* of having.

Imagine that the life your Soul designed was to be experienced on a wide open, abundant, rolling green pasture, extending from horizon to horizon, with plenty of sun and shade, fresh living water and nourishing food. Yet, because of your ego-mind training, you may find yourself fenced inside a dusty corral with brackish water and tumbling tumbleweeds. In that corral of misperception your ego-mind shows signs of distress. It is imbalanced, creating negative behaviors out of apathy, fear or rebelliousness.

An ego-mind that has given up and no longer cares about the Soul's purpose is like an apathetic horse lying in the dirt. It may be right next to the fence, with the luscious pasture just a short distance away. Yet, it ignores the Soul's prodding and encouragement and remains suffering, feeling disempowered or uninterested, and unwilling to make the effort to jump the fence.

Sometimes the ego-mind becomes fearful. It desires the green pasture and feels drawn toward it. However, its fear holds it back. It has great power, yet it shies away from the rich opportunities just over the fence. It feels trapped and anxious. It may rear up and try to buck the Soul when prodded to jump. It resists the promptings and recoils when the Soul spurs it onward. And so, unwilling to overcome its fear, it too remains within the corral of its programming.

When the ego-mind is rebellious it makes a conscious choice to reject the Soul's guidance. It will buck, kick, bite, twist, turn and do all it can to unseat the Soul. It will drag the Soul through the dirt and mud. It claims to prefer the tumbleweeds, dirt, and brackish water. Every prodding of the Soul is met with rejection and refusal, and it remains convinced of the illusion of freedom within the corral of false beliefs.

Soul Authority

A horse requires a balanced life of regular exercise, mental discipline and positive attention to live happily with a human. It needs leadership from a trainer who is energetically calm and assertive.[ii] Without this, a horse will show symptoms of imbalance such as fear, anxiety or aggression.

When a trainer provides for a horse's real needs, and is energetically calm and in charge, the horse feels the trainer's authority and can relax and enjoy life.[iii] A master trainer understands that energy is the true Universal language of all living creatures, and it is the flow of positive, calm and assertive energy that brings peace.[iv] They communicate directly with the Soul.

Most of us have an ego-mind that is like an improperly trained horse, corralled with the tumbleweeds and lacking proper care and attention. Like an imbalanced horse, your ego-mind may show signs of distress when your acquired beliefs are not in alignment with your Soul's plans. While your early trainers may not have taught you properly, and you accumulated further false beliefs through your misperceptions, you can complete the task of retraining yourself.

Your mind needs the discipline of focused meditation to calm down, relax and listen. When you relax your ego-mind and align with your Soul, you connect with your innate calm, centered confidence. Once your ego-mind is still, you can feel the peace derived from your Soul's leadership. It is in this stillness that you can hear the voice of your Soul. Then, you can be in this world with purpose, meaning and clear direction from within.

Using your inner guidance, you are capable of identifying your negative programs and taming your ego-mind, bringing it onto the path of your Soul's true design. You can then experience the real freedom of your Soul, mind and body moving in unison. The Ancient Ones call this the *Soul Self* – the harmony of the body, ego-mind and Soul, when the Soul is in charge. It is the Soul Self that jumps the fence, leaves the corral and thrives in the green meadows of life.

A Successful Voyage

Another way to imagine the Soul/ego-mind/body relationship is through the example of a ship's crew. The captain is in command and is responsible for making wise decisions for the highest good of the ship. On a well-run ship, the captain is aware of the larger picture and the available options, so that correct decisions can be made. The captain then informs the chief mate. The chief mate is second in command, handling the management of day-to-day activities, such as the maintenance and logistics of the ship. He or she brings vital problems to the captain for consideration, and has the job of listening to the directives of the captain, passing them on to the sailors, then making sure that those orders are carried out. When the system is running smoothly, and everyone is working in cooperation, then the ship remains on course, and the crew completes the voyage without damage or delay.

Your Soul is the captain of your ship, of your life. With your Soul in charge, you are able to make decisions that are wise, because they are in accordance with your life purpose. When you accept your intrinsic inner authority, you can make decisions that are rooted in powerful insight, vision, clarity, and strength. Your ego-mind can be an excellent manager, like the chief mate — full of knowledge and capable of getting things done. It can execute the directives of your Soul, by adjusting your thoughts and moving your body to accomplish what is needed. This is possible because the direction given by the Soul always includes the next step, every day, every moment, in every choice.

When the ego-mind accepts the leadership of the Soul, doors begin to open. The right people show up to assist, needs are met, and next opportunities are evident. Life moves forward in positive experiences, one right after the other. With the ego-mind in line with the Soul, the body moves naturally into alignment.

Because of the training and outside programming that we have received, most of us have allowed our chief mate to push our captain aside, and a mutiny is in progress. This rebellion has likely led to choices we have made without utilizing our full wisdom. We may be wondering, "How did I end up in this mess? How did I get here? I wanted to sail to Tahiti, so what am I doing in Madagascar?!"

Misdirection happens when the real leader is not in charge of our ship. It can be taken off course and sent somewhere unintended. The chief mate is an excellent sailor, but he or she is not likely to complete the journey successfully without direction from the true leader, who understands the purpose for the voyage. You can choose whether to respect the leadership of the captain or join in the mutiny of the chief mate. You are always at choice.

Locating the Ego Mind

Ask yourself the following question. (However, before you think of the answer, give yourself a moment to let your answer arise within and feel what happens):

"Where in my body do I feel fear, anger, or embarrassment?"

Pause now to notice the feelings, and where you feel them. Take your time. Note your answers.

Do you feel the energy behind the feelings? What is your body telling you? Do you have a sense of contraction, heaviness or discomfort? Can you identify where these feelings are residing? If you give it enough time, you will know for yourself a Universal phenomenon: the negative feelings of the ego-mind reside in the solar plexus, the 3rd chakra. The negative feelings of the belly reveal themselves in many common idioms. Has a frightening or embarrassing experience ever made you feel "sick to your stomach"? Have you ever said, or heard someone else say, in anger or resentment, "I hate his guts!"? When anxious, have you felt "butterflies in your tummy"? Have you had a sinking feeling in the "pit of your belly" when hearing bad news? This is where the ego-mind lives, and these are some of the negative expressions associated with it.

The ego is powerful and forceful but it is not intended to direct our choices. When your ego is driving your decisions, you may experience negative feelings much longer than necessary, which will create difficulties in your life if you do not address them immediately. It is not our negative experiences that bring about negative thoughts and feelings. Rather, it is our negative feelings and thoughts that create our negative experiences. When you feel out of balance mentally, emotionally or physically, the experiences you create reflect this.

The Soul Center

You can observe within yourself that when you feel mentally, emotionally and physically positive, your life experiences are likely to turn out the way you desire. Your positive feelings indicate that you are moving in the right direction. When you feel affectionate, confident, engaged, inspired, excited, exhilarated, grateful, hopeful, joyful, peaceful or refreshed, you enjoy yourself and experience fulfillment.[v] Feelings like these express the qualities of the Soul.

> Now, ask yourself the following question and allow the answer to come to you:
>
> *"Where in my body do I feel love, joy, fulfillment and happiness?"*
>
> Pause now to notice where you feel these feelings. Take your time. Make note of your answer.

Do you feel the energy behind the feelings? What is your body telling you? Do you feel expansive, empowered or energized? Can you identify where these feelings reside?

If you give it enough time, you will recognize another Universal phenomenon: the positive feelings of your Soul reside in your heart center, the 4th Chakra. Your Soul expresses through your heart, and this is why the heart center is sometimes called the Soul center. It is no accident that the picture symbol for both love and the heart are the same, because real love lives in the heart center. So do joy, happiness, hope, and the many other life- affirming feelings of the Soul. This is also where you experience your inner *knowing*, your wisdom, with clarity and accuracy.

Heart-Centered Decisions

Imagine that you have a dilemma. A choice needs to be made, and action needs to be taken. If you want to have more clarity about the distinction between the ego-mind and the Soul, it may be helpful to visualize it like this:

Ego-mind/Belly/3rd Chakra	**Soul/Heart/4th Chakra**
Knowledge	*Knowing*
Figuring it out	Feeling what is
Looking for an answer	Allowing the answer to emerge
Feeling stress, anxiety, pressure	Feeling serenity, peace, relief
Thinking it cannot be done	Trusting my guidance to show me the way
Following the formula or the training	Creating in the moment
"I made a commitment, so I have to do it."	"I changed my mind because I know differently now."
"What will people think?"	"What do I know to be true for me?"

Real Love

Real love is expressed from the heart center. This is not to be confused with the kind of love that is syrupy sweet and comes with contracts, terms and conditions. That is sentimentality, which expresses from the belly. Real love does not have ulterior motives. It is not deserved or earned, and it is not a reward for being a good girl or boy. Real love is. It endures. Real love loves no matter what.

Maybe as a child you had a relative or a friend who loved you unconditionally. When you were in his or her presence you felt it, you just knew you were loved. He or she loved you just because you were you. That is love without conditions. That is real love.

Now here's a big question: Can you love yourself like that? Can you love yourself just because you are YOU?

When you experience your life from your heart center, when you make that place your home, you demonstrate that you truly love yourself. As real love becomes your foundation, you can heal your wounds, unleash your passions, and express your individual genius. And, in sharing all of that with others, you can remind those around you that they too are expressions of real love. You become a source of hope, inspiration and integrity.

The Library of the Mind

Remaining in your heart becomes easier when you realize that your ego-mind is only a repository of information. Like a library that holds a collection of books, it is full of knowledge. Everything you have ever learned resides in the library of your ego-mind. It can retain facts, figures, and memories of past experiences. It can hold gossip, judgment and opinion. Every ego- mind contains past knowledge that is no longer current, or alive.

The training your ego-mind received from others, the knowledge you have acquired through your experiences, and the beliefs based upon your interpretation of your experiences are like various books you have added to your library. Your ego-mind holds an amazing quantity of remembered detail, and it can be a remarkably useful tool. However, it does not know how to distinguish between truth and untruth, fact and fiction, what is real and what is imagined.[vi] It is a resource to draw upon, but it cannot tell you your unique purpose or the next step of your life's true path.

Because of your negative programming, much of what you think you know may be false![vii] Almost any idea or concept that you believe could be wrong! A travel book can describe much about a place you may wish to visit, but the recommendations in even the best tourist guidebooks are based upon someone else's past experience, not what is happening now. The information may have been true for the person writing it, at the time they wrote it. However, when you make the journey yourself, you may find that the information is no longer accurate. Like an outdated travel book, your ego-mind is unreliable without your Soul's guidance. Why rely on old information?

There is much in life that the ego-mind cannot predict, anticipate or comprehend. Have you ever thoroughly analyzed a problem, strategized ways to solve it, and after acting on your solution the results still turned out badly? Even after all of that preparation? It was likely the unforeseen problems that derailed the progress of your desired outcome. So, you crashed head-on into the limitations of your ego-mind. Operating alone, your ego-mind makes choices based on what was in order to determine what *could be*. It only knows what is in its library. It cannot know what is not there. And, even what is there may be wrong! Remember this: our ego-minds are designed to *follow* direction, not give it.

Soul Freedom

Your Soul is not limited by the library of your ego-mind. Just as the make-up of a drop of sea-water is indistinguishable from the ocean from which it came, so too your Soul is of the same substance as the whole of divinity. It is already aware of the opportunities that are available, and it can clear the blocked pathways your ego-mind cannot perceive.

Recall a time when you could not figure out the answer to a problem no matter how hard you tried, but you just *knew in your heart* that if you were to act on your hunch everything would turn out all right…and it did! You could not explain it. You just did it, and it worked! Later, when you analyzed what happened, perhaps you discovered that an unpredictable chain of circumstances came into alignment in a seemingly miraculous way, and you achieved your goal.

Perhaps you once experienced a moment of creativity when you lost the sense of time because you were feeling so much joy. Can you remember a time when you were playing a sport, performing music, making love or engaged in some other activity when your perception of reality shifted? Time slowed, and everything around you became crystal clear. Ideas of trying to *do* it left your mind, and you just *were* it. You were the sport, the music, the lovemaking, the activity itself. There was no separation between how you felt and what you did. While you could not explain it, neither could you deny that something exceptional had occurred.

How did these magic moments happen? You shifted from trying, into allowing! You allowed the flow of life-force energy, the Universe, divinity, love and grace to flow through you. In other words, you became inseparable from this flow. You became one with the flow. You were an embodied expression of life-force energy, your ego-mind surrendered and your Soul's *knowing* emerged. You experienced an immersion in the awareness of what *is*.

Rather than thinking, trying or denying, you can allow your wisdom to flow, so you speak, move, and relate with what is happening now. Instead of *reacting* to what is perceived, you may enter into a state of grace. You can let your knowing, your truth, prevail over the falsehoods. As Jesus the Christ taught, "the truth will set you free."[viii] It is your knowing, your inner truth, and acceptance of your own light, love and unique, divine expression that will set you free from the tyranny of the limited, programmed mind. Then, you can enjoy true freedom of the Soul.

Soul freedom is living in the eye of the storm. While the world of the ego may be raging, howling and blowing all around, in your center, your truth, all is calm, clear and at peace. From your Soul center, you can see that you are creating your life with every thought and every choice, and you can decide to rise into a higher perspective. To live in Soul freedom is a choice: you can live in love, calm, peace and clarity, or, you can choose to live in judgment, fear, resentment and distortion. You can live from your heart or your belly. You can experience life as guided by your Soul or directed by your ego-mind. You always have a choice, and you are always at choice.

Our Feelings Are Indicators

If you want to evolve consciously out of the chaos around you, you are going to have to go out of your mind. This requires practice and diligence. Old habits can be difficult to change. Start simply, in meditation. Quietly ask your Soul a question within. Pay attention to where you feel your answer. You may wish to touch your heart lightly, as a reminder of where your true answer is to appear. One way of accessing your knowing is through your feelings, so practice asking questions and noticing how you feel.

When you are in your heart center, you can experience negative emotions without allowing them to control you. For example, you can experience anger yet not be angry. You can be the observer of the anger, noticing it from your calm, peaceful center. Experienced in this way, your anger can be useful rather than destructive. In any situation, when you feel a negative emotion, this is a crucial moment. Your Soul is saying, "Stay present and pay attention!"

You can tell whether you are following your inner guidance by how you feel, and where you feel it. Listen to your body. If you are feeling contracted, irritated or off-balance, these are indicators that you have been pulled out of your heart center. It is usually destructive to remain in extended periods of negative feelings such as fear, annoyance, anger, sadness or tension.[ix] The moment you notice any of these negative feelings within you, bring your attention back into your heart center. You might say to yourself, "Wow! I'm feeling anger! I recognize this is a warning for me to pay attention. Something needs to change. OK, what do I need to know or do now?" Stay with that question until you begin to feel relief, expansion and inner-balance.

When you allow your answers to rise into your heart, you can get the full *knowing* of what to do next, of how to proceed. Then you can prepare and act from your inner wisdom. Look how much trouble you can save! By getting present with what is, you remain peacefully and calmly in real love. You do not react or make more trouble. Your inner knowing can come through clearly and accurately, so that you can act properly. This is applying *wisdom*.

Upgrading Your Library

Wisdom means you are responding to what is, now. Wisdom is listening to your truth, your knowing, your Soul – which is alive! Wisdom is not in your ego-mind; knowledge is there. However, you can improve your library! If you like a belief you can keep it. If you prefer not to, that's your choice. It is up to you to decide what you want to know, believe and accept as yours. Spiritual teachers throughout the ages have taught what science is now showing: it is possible to discard the outdated books, the negative thoughts and beliefs, and replace them with more useful ones.[x]

You do this by first, changing your attitude. You can choose healthy, vibrant, joyful, life-affirming information to put into your mind. Then, when you want to use the library, the information there is constructive. It is easier to apply inner wisdom when you are drawing from the shelves of positive knowledge instead of the discard bins of negative, outdated beliefs.

The voice of your Soul is the voice of your divinity, and it speaks your individual truth. Your truth, or *knowing*, lives within you, and it has all of your answers, including why you are here, why you have had the experiences in your life thus far, and where you are going next. It holds the blueprint of your life, and navigational instructions to stay on course each and every moment.

When you rise into your Soul center and stay there, a marvelous experience begins to open up. In addition to feeling serenity and peace, you also feel trust. You ease up. Your belly relaxes and your hearts open further. You feel confidence in your Self, your path and your inner knowing. Not only because you begin to see the results of your knowing, but because you *know that you know*. That is so much more effective than wondering if you know, or thinking that you know (when you actually do not), or getting lucky, or waiting for a miracle. When you know that you know you can have a confident awareness and understanding of what truly matters.

As you follow your inner wisdom, you enter into a Self-assured knowingness of your purpose. You discover that your Soul designs experiences that will assist you to fulfill this purpose. You enjoy the freedom of following your bliss, which is your true path. You enjoy more love, wisdom and passion. You know that you can create your future through the positive interpretation of what is happening in any moment. This knowing blossoms naturally into trust in your Soul's guidance, which directs you onto your path, into joy and into the experiences that allow you to fulfill your true desires.

Staying in the Saddle

> If you would like to experience life from your heart center, right now you can say:
>
> *"I now choose to live in my heart center, in peace and divine clarity."*
>
> Touch your heart if you like. Allow the feelings of lightness, peacefulness, and expansion to grow within you. Stay with these feelings as long and as often as you can, and this statement will become true for you!

This feeling of heart-centeredness will remain until you encounter a distraction or interruption – which is likely to happen soon! That disturbance could be a negative thought or feeling. Someone might say something to you and your reaction pulls you off center.

It is always the ego-mind that reacts, and it can be as powerful as a bucking bronco. This may have happened so often in your past that you have grown accustomed to your negative behavior, and you may not realize that you have been tossed down into the mud.

If you find yourself wallowing in the world of opinion, gossip and judgment, then you have dropped into your belly. You may be angry, critical, or judging of yourself or another. Those behaviors are not YOU; they are the reactions of your ego-mind. Take a moment and breathe. Relax. Bring your awareness back up into your heart and choose again to remain there.

The choice is yours. If you find yourself in the mud, with your horse dragging you by the stirrups, then you must get back in the saddle, and determine to stay on. If you are to master your ego-mind you must get out of your belly and rise into your heart!

Apply the Wisdom

Like learning a musical instrument or a new language, learning to distinguish between the ego-mind and the Soul requires practice. Get to know yourself, see if you can recognize whether your thoughts are originating in your heart or belly. Practice bringing your awareness into your heart center, and feeling the difference between knowledge and knowing. You may easily notice where some feelings and thoughts are originating, while others are more difficult. This is natural and to be expected at first. Do not be discouraged. Keep at it! Your effort will be rewarded. Remember that everything can be experienced more clearly when you bring it into your heart.

Pebbles: A Fable

At the base of a beautiful, lofty mountain peak, in a hidden little valley, dwelled a bustling village. In this village, the people passed their days in an unusual pastime. Each person carried a bucket in his or her hand at all times and kept a pocket or a little purse full of pebbles. Every day, the villagers went to market, their place of work, or to visit with their neighbors. When they told an idea or a belief, right or wrong, they would take a pebble out of their purse or pocket, and drop it into the bucket of the person to whom they were speaking.

The people in this village did not actually know much about the world. They kept within the boundaries of their village, and no outside visitors knew to find them. Still, the villagers felt sure of what the world was like, the nature of God and the Universe, who made the best bread in the village, etc. Of course, every villager had a different opinion about these things, but each one felt convinced that he or she was right. Now having a bucket full of pebbles was a sign of greatness and knowledge, so no one ever emptied his or her bucket. As the days, months and years passed some buckets got to be extra heavy.

One day, a young girl felt inspired to leave the village, to go discover what she could see from the top of the nearby mountain peak. No one had ever been there before because people were busy collecting pebbles. Some had tried, but their buckets were so heavy that they would grow tired and quit, or they were afraid that their hearts would give out! In time, nobody bothered trying anymore. Unlike the others, this girl decided she would make it to the top of the mountain.

She set out early that morning to get a fresh start. Though she was young, and her bucket was only partly full, it was still quite heavy, and she had to walk slowly. As the sun rose, her family and neighbors discovered that she had left, and they could faintly see her as a small spot moving up the side of the mountain. They filled one another's buckets with opinions and judgments about her, and had to replenish their pockets and purses just to get through the gossip before lunchtime!

Meanwhile, the girl had climbed into the heat of the day, her heavy bucket dragging along beside her. Under a shade tree, near a cool brook, she thought, "my journey will be easier if I take some of these pebbles out of my bucket." This proved difficult because each pebble represented an idea or belief that she had accepted. Some of them she doubted were true, but she felt soothed by them, so she kept them. She kept nearly all of them, but she did find three ideas she was willing to let go of and so she removed three pebbles.

She continued her climb and found that as she gained height up the mountain she could see that some of her ideas and beliefs simply were not true! Hers was not the only valley in the world, for example. She could see two others! She discovered a flower growing that someone had told her was extinct! She had the courage to climb – her heart had not quit and neither had she! With each new insight, she took out more pebbles.

The climb grew steeper and rockier, but she held firm in her determination to make it to the top. As she climbed, her bucket banged noisily against the rocks. It had been heavy in the beginning, but it was getting amazingly lighter as she went on alone. Onward she hiked into the cloud cover.

Sometime in the late afternoon, as she rested on the crest of a great boulder, she noticed something she could not remember seeing before. Her bucket was empty! Looking into the bottom of the bucket, she saw the holes that the jagged rocks made when she had banged her bucket against them during her climb. Her pebbles had all spilled out!

The girl had a moment of regret. "How will I remember my ideas and beliefs now?" she cried. Through her tears, she saw the clouds parting below her. As she looked around, she realized that she was sitting on top of the mountain! She had a view of the land as it truly was. It was spectacular! Her village in the valley lay below her, and beyond it she could see even higher mountains with valleys between. Perhaps there were even more villages!

She then knew in her heart that very few of the pebbles that had been put in her bucket were true for her. The truths she discovered on her own – from her own effort – were more real! She only needed to get a high enough perspective!

She delighted in the pleasure of her accomplishment and knowing that she was now done with the bucket, she set it down. She felt truly free and happy to journey home without the burden of her inherited beliefs. Smiling joyfully, she headed down the mountain to share with others what she had just attained.

> "The climb grew steeper and rockier, but she held firm in her determination to make it to the top."

From The Ancient Ones: The Human Make-Up

The human make-up is simple when approached scientifically. Each person is born with a physical body that operates automatically, without the need to be manually directed to breathe, digest, repair or grow. All of these functions happen on their own.

Each person comes equipped with a mind to think, communicate and create. This part of the human is called the Ego. It has likes and dislikes; it can be developed in many differing ways. The personality is made up of numerous characteristics, which are developed through training, or by default or lack of direction. This Ego-mind responds according to the way it is programmed.

The Soul of each human has a "blueprint" or reason for their particular incarnation. This purpose is their unique drive or passion. When one has discovered their passion in life, they awaken to the ever present beauty of life on Earth. Joy is their main experience, and they are filled with enthusiasm for living.

The final part of the equation is the life-force or Spirit which is flowing through every living organism on this planet. We are each endowed with this pulsating energy. How much we open to its constant flow is up to us. More life flow equals greater expression of joy, love, life.

People who have not yet found their own truth or intention many times find themselves despondent or lacking real passion for living. They end up either following someone else's dream or they hide away in their solitude. Neither way brings true fulfillment. Our desire is to assist each one who is willing to find their purpose, passion, and true joy in life. Soul Self Living is aimed to this actualization.

2

Finding Your True Voice

Maintaining your heart-centered focus can be challenging at times, but it becomes easier when you realize that it all begins with your attitude. When you combine your positive thoughts and pleasing feelings you create an uplifting force that vibrates in harmony with the supportive forces of creation. As a piano tuner uses a tuning fork to bring a piano string into resonance, your gracious attitude allows your ego-mind to come into alignment with your Soul. This creates an attractive force that builds positivity, which enables you to sit firmly in your Soul center.

Your attitude affects your choices, which affect the outcome of your actions. By maintaining an affirmative outlook, you are telling your ego-mind that your Soul is in charge. You remember that no one outside of you controls your thoughts or feelings. Taking full charge of your thoughts and feelings means you can enjoy more positive flow of life-force energy in your life, express your divinity and make decisions that are in alignment with your purpose.

At first you may seek to benefit from inspiring music, books, affirmations or a skilled coach. The Soul is always positive and resonates with external inputs such as these. Eventually, as your heart becomes your home, your ego-mind naturally falls into alignment and balance; the horse and rider find their rhythm. This opens the way for uncovering your blueprint and finding your true voice.

The Soul's Knowing

Jesuit philosopher Pierre Teilhard de Chardin wrote, "We are spiritual beings having a human experience."[xi] By recognizing your spiritual nature, you open up to a larger aspect of yourself than your physical and mental expressions. You honor your Soul.

Your Soul is the larger, eternal aspect of yourself that exists before you incarnate, is still with you through your lifetime, and that endures after your physical death. You may perceive your Soul as wisdom deep within you that extends beyond your ego-mind and body. You may feel or sense your Soul as inner knowing, or hear it as a still, small voice emerging from inside you.

While your ego is limited by your physical senses and mental processes, your Soul does not have such restrictions. It is aware of your purpose, your circumstances (from a much greater perspective), and your possibilities. The Soul is not limited by the physical concept of time and so, when you listen carefully within, you can expand your understanding of your past and present, and even gain awareness of your potential future.

Life-Force Energy

Life-force energy, or Spirit, is flowing through every living organism on Earth, and your Soul is always immersed in, and connected to, this eternal Source. Life-force is synonymous with real love, which is unconditional and powerfully constant. While your ego may have been trained to believe that you must earn the right to accept this flow, from your Souls perspective, you can realize that real love is not earned or deserved. It is always available. You need only allow yourself to experience it.

Real love is felt in your heart, and it is through your heart that it can stream abundantly through every cell of your body and every aspect of your Being. Your heart is like a floodgate, and it is up to you to keep it open so that your life is nourished with an infinite flow of love. When you allow Spirit to flow unimpeded through your whole Being, it is like irrigation water flooding a parched field, restoring life and vitality to the land. At any time, you can open your heart and let that love, peace, beauty, and joy surge forth.

Life-force energy sustains, nourishes and protects us. As you cultivate your positive attitude your positive feeling can take root, and you can feel them more deeply. This creates a feedback loop of positivity that builds a greater and greater sense of empowerment, fulfillment and purpose within us.

When you cultivate positivity you develop into the embodiment of life-sustaining energy your Soul intended in your design. The more you allow life-force energy to enliven you, the more surplus you have to share with others. You mature from programmed ego-mind living, feeling disconnected and isolated (or codependent and controlled), into a real, independent and interconnected human being.

"Your heart is like a floodgate, and it is up to you to keep it open so that your life is nourished with an infinite flow of love."

The Pond of Perception

Take a moment now to bring your awareness into your heart center. Place your hand there if you like. Imagine that you are high up in pristine mountains observing yourself as a clear, still pond fed by an underground spring of fresh water deep below. Notice your depth, purity and translucence. See the sunlight sparkling on your surface. Enjoy a deep cleansing breath or two of sweet mountain air and simply allow yourself to feel completely at ease. Allow stillness and quiet to grow within your heart, and release all else. Let yourself feel held in peace.

As you relax, you may accept that all is well in this moment, now. You may want to say that out loud to anchor it:

"All is well in this moment, now"

Imagine the current of the pure spring rising from deep within the pond, and feel the current of life-force energy flowing through your heart, imbuing you with love, peace, and grace. Expand this feeling into a deeper sense of serenity and harmony throughout your mind and body, and appreciate that your knowing is becoming clearer and more accurate with every breath.

As your mind and body become still, allow your Soul to reveal itself through you, while reflecting back to your ego-mind the truth of your Self: your divine origin, pure heart and inner strength.

Continue to feel the enlivening tranquility you have opened up within yourself. Allow this feeling to settle around and over you. Let your meditation become a mirror – to deeply reflect your truth back to you. Enjoy the feeling of expansion within your heart center. As you dissolve into peacefulness, lucidity and calm attentiveness, let your inner knowing emerge, and uncover the guidance that is there for you.

Cultivating a Relationship with Your Self

Utilize the Pond of Perception exercise to cultivate a relationship with your Self. Begin a habit of inner dialog with your Soul. Explore your innate wisdom and enjoy the process of uncovering your truth! Go into your heart center, ask lots of questions and get your own answers. All of your answers are there. It is in your heart space that wisdom lives. When you live in your heart, you experience who you actually are – beyond the stories you tell yourself, or the stories other people have about you. You can experience the truth of your reality and see that you are now, and have always been, at choice – about what to think, how to behave, when to act, and where to be. You can gain an understanding of why you had made certain decisions in the past, and what factors are priorities in your present choices.

All that Spirit flowing through your open heart center enlivens your inner perception, and creates the proper internal environment for wisdom to be expressed in your outer circumstances. You are able to be wise when you receive your answers from within. In time, you will come to trust this wisdom because you enjoy the accuracy of our insights, the surety of your choices and the positive effects of your actions. It is in the manifestation of your true desires that you especially appreciate the benefits of your inner knowing.

By listening within and developing a relationship with your Self, you will get to know yourself pretty well. And, the more you get to know yourself, the more you will grow to love yourself, which is essential!

Have you ever had a true friend, who loved you no matter what? Who was willing to tell you what he or she honestly thought? Who was willing to help you see what you were unable or unwilling to acknowledge on your own? As good as that felt, your relationship with your true Self is even greater because your Soul is an expression of unconditional love.

Your Soul is the best kind of friend you will ever know. It will never give you an opinion (that is the job of the ego-mind). It will only give you your truth. If it is in your highest good to know the answer to your question, your Soul will tell you. Every time! It will direct you in the manner you most need in any given moment. You may be gently encouraged by your Soul, or sternly warned. Sometimes the guidance is like a whisper and, at other times, you may even feel as if your Soul is shouting to you! It will give you the best advice – accurate, honest and just for you.

You can always count on the integrity of your inner counsel. Sometimes the answer to your question will be a simple "yes", "no" or "not yet." At other times you can receive volumes of information. You may not always *like* what you hear. Sometimes the guidance you receive may appear too difficult or painful to follow. You may cringe or feel the temptation to say, "Forget that!" Yet, if you listen and follow your inner guidance, trust your personal relationship with your truest Self, and follow those directions you will live a much richer, fuller, more fulfilling and joyous life.

As you ask questions, receive answers, and then ask more clarifying questions, you are building a relationship with your Self. The best relationships are founded upon trust. Do you know how amazing it is to truly trust yourself? To have no more guessing, worrying or wondering about the accuracy of your decisions? Make the time each day to cultivate a true friendship with your Soul, and discover the joyful life that is your birthright.

Why Wait?

You are learning, growing and evolving, and you may now be doing this more consciously than you did at earlier times in your life. When you can appreciate this truth, then you can make another, higher shift in consciousness. When you recognize where you have been relative to where you are now, then you make the shift from ignorance into awareness.

There have been many accounts of people who have returned to life after a near-death experience. Some of them have described "seeing their life pass before their eyes," or re-experiencing the significant events of their incarnation, in detail, with perfect awareness of the lessons learned.[xii] With clear communication within, there is no need to wait until after death for a full life review. Right now, you can ask your Soul questions about earlier periods in your life, and apply the insights to your present situation.

As you develop your inner dialog, you may come into some startling revelations about your behavior. You may discover things about your life, choices you made, and ways you had been relating that, from your new awareness, you can clearly see were not healthy choices for you. In some cases, you may feel shocked to discover the sources of your negative situations. You may identify errors you had made that you previously thought were careful decisions! Be courageous! Face the truth. In seeing it, you can begin taking responsibility for your past and present choices from a higher perspective.

In reviewing a situation, don't put yourself into the past. Rather, bring the experience into the present moment, within the heart center. Remain objective. Be the observer of the situation, rather than the participant. In doing this, you can revisit every skeleton you have hidden in your mental/emotional closets (even the ones you may have hoped to forget forever). In your heart center, in real love, you can go through those closets and clean them out. You can examine *anything* you have done in the past and see what happened from a higher perspective. You can review why you made certain decisions and what beliefs you based them upon. You can see how things might have turned out differently if you had made different choices, and you can replace those outdated beliefs.

You raise your consciousness by asking for wisdom to emerge from your knowledge. When you learn from an experience, it is essential that you not compartmentalize that lesson by applying it to only that situation. Ask to be shown where you can use the new understanding you have gained. Examine how you can improve your present circumstances with this new awareness, and diligently do so.

True wisdom is applying your insights into every area and facet of your life. Trusting your innate wisdom and acting on your inner guidance allows your life to unfold in accordance with your Soul's intentions. Utilizing your past experiences to learn from your Soul's perspective, helps you to gain greater understanding of your present circumstances. You can feel more clarity about your current options, and make wiser choices. By learning from your insights you can make a fresh start with new resolve. This is the foundational work of transmuting knowledge into wisdom.

Positive Interpretation

When reviewing your past decisions, you may struggle with negative thoughts or feelings such as despair, loneliness, guilt, blame, anger, or self-condemnation. These feelings are invitations to pay attention. Feel your feelings from your heart center, and do your best to observe them with detachment. Notice your feelings without identifying yourself *as* them. Utilize those negative thoughts or feelings to identify their sources, and express them fully, but resist the temptation to linger in them. This will help you remain in your *Soul reality*. Through inner dialog, the lessons inside the experiences that produced those feelings can be learned thoroughly and safely. Insight, vision, clarity and constructive resolution can naturally emerge.

Sometimes, the ego-mind reacts to what it thinks is a negative situation and bucks you down into *ego reality*. Nearly every human being has the tendency to slip down off their horse to wallow in their negative feelings from time to time. However, remaining in negativity is like staying in the mud after falling from a horse! It stinks! It is uncomfortable! Even painful! It can also be intensely difficult to get back up.

Continuing to immerse in the emotions of the belly can make you feel stuck or stagnant, because you are! If you are down in the mud, you are not riding forward. Fortunately, your struggling stops when you change your attitude, decide to pull yourself up out of the mud and get back up into your heart where the rider, your Soul, is in charge.

The key to shifting from the ego-mind to the heart is finding the positive interpretation of any occurrence that is bringing, or has brought about, negative thoughts or feelings. If you want to have clarity about how to proceed with wisdom, you must bring your awareness into your heart center, and remain positive about whatever you are going through. Energetically, this is like taking a shower, washing off the mud and returning to calm, clear centeredness.

Raising Consciousness

When you were a baby someone held, carried and cared for you. Because you were constantly with them, you experienced the reality that your parents or caregivers created for themselves. You lived in a world created by other people and depended upon those who cared for you.

In time, you learned to crawl, walk, feed yourself, dress without help and gradually experience self-reliance to a greater extent. You learned that you could affect reality by your choices because your actions had consequences. You discovered personal preferences about what you liked to eat, wear, and do.

Most of us challenged our caregivers by pushing for our independence, and we eventually gained our full autonomy and supported ourselves. Hopefully, we then learned to care for others and appreciate our interdependence with everyone and everything else.

As a mature adult, you are responsible for everything that happens in your life, consciously or unconsciously. You are not a victim of life, for you create your life through your choices. There is nothing outside of you making your decisions for you. You need not look outside of yourself because the answer is always within.

Yet, even as an adult, with careful observation, you can humbly recognize that you are probably still growing up in one way or another. Your Soul's aim is for you is to fully mature into the natural, balanced, wise and capable human being that you came here to be, and this requires higher levels of consciousness than you may have previously experienced.

Consciousness has levels, and we all have our present level of consciousness. Your level of consciousness determines how you identify with yourself, and life. It is the way you view your life in this moment, including your opinions and beliefs. One definition can be "what we pay attention to." At the kindergarten level, we pay attention to ABC's and 123's. At the post-graduate level, we pay attention to designing new realities.

You rise into higher levels of consciousness by raising your perspective. From a higher inner vantage point you pay attention to different things. If you were to view yourself within the larger landscape of the entirety of your life experience, you would begin to notice more than what you experience within the framework of a single day. You would notice more than you do with your physical senses. You could observe the inner chatter of your ego-mind objectively. You could view the way you interact with others, the states of mind you are in when you relate with them, and the different belief systems that influence your perceptions and actions. You could gain insights from this higher perspective and apply them to make more informed choices.

When you access your inner wisdom through inner dialog with your Soul, you gain a deeper understanding of yourself, why you have made past decisions, and what beliefs are informing your current ones. You can utilize these insights to set new intentions. You can change your beliefs, make new choices, and determine a course of action today that will bring you your future desires. In short, you can make wiser decisions.

As you raise your consciousness, you begin to understand that your experience is your creation. When you truly appreciate the power of your creativity, you can take full responsibility for your life. You can learn from your past choices, let go of old programs and enjoy the best qualities of your Self. You can treasure your Soul insights as well as your ego-mind skills, and bring them into alignment and balance. Instead of struggling through ego experiences you don't want, you can rise into your Soul's higher perspective and relish the life you truly desire. You can experience joy, grace and fulfillment, and celebrate the variety of opportunities available on this beautiful, abundant planet in which you live.

It is possible to raise your individual consciousness enough to have a tangible comprehension of the reality that you are an integral part of *All That Is*. With this larger awareness, you support increasing consciousness on the planet with greater affect. As a conscious co-creator of your life, you naturally become a leader, an example and source of inspiration for others. And, the feedback loop of positivity you create within you extends beyond the boundaries of your individual expression as it connects with everything in existence.

Forgiveness

Forgiveness is another key to raising your consciousness. It is essential for the maturing of each aspect of yourself from dependence, to independence to interdependence. You must be willing to forgive the ignorance of your old ego ways.

When you were in high school learning algebra, trigonometry or calculus you did not think, "I was such an idiot for not learning this in kindergarten or first grade!" or "I cannot believe that my teacher back then did not teach this to me!" So why then would you beat yourself up emotionally or blame others for the things you did not achieve, or did not know because of the level of consciousness you were in at that time?

Remember that a higher level of consciousness means having a higher perspective. When you are willing to learn from your experiences and accept the lessons within them, you expand your consciousness even further. In your wisdom, you know that the experience was necessary in order to learn and grow. Therefore, now you can forgive yourself, where you could not before.

The Process of Forgiveness

1. Ask within to be shown an event from your life that still requires forgiveness of yourself and that you are ready to forgive. Maybe it is something you said to someone, a decision you regret and have not let go of, or a silent judgment you made about yourself or someone else.

When you are ready ask within: *"Have I taken responsibility for my part?"*

2. Are you seeing yourself as a victim? Are you blaming another? Or, are you accepting that you did what you did, what's done is done, and that you are responsible for your decisions and actions?

When you can, say, *"I take responsibility for my part."*

3. Are you trying to push the issue away, hide from it or suppress it? Are you hoping to move on quickly without a full appreciation of why you acted? Or, have you learned from the experience? Have you gained understanding or awareness from what happened?

Take a moment to ask within, *"What have I learned from this experience?"*

4. Allow the insights to emerge, the wisdom to reveal itself. Remember to choose the positive interpretation. This makes every

experience useful. Mine the gold from it. Glean every bit of value from what happened.

When you feel that you can honestly do so, say, "*I have learned my lesson.*"

5. Because you have learned your lesson, you can now apply it. You can make a different choice now, and benefit from knowing that if you could do it all over again, you would act differently.

When you are able to do so, say, "*I can make a different choice now.*"

6. What choice would you make now? Can you imagine how the situation might have been different if you had done otherwise? If a similar situation occurs in the future, will you act differently then? Can you see that you have taken responsibility, learned your lesson and made a new decision that is from a higher level of consciousness? By doing so, now you can take the final, and necessary step.

When you are ready, say, "*I can now forgive myself.*"

7. Take a deep breath and allow the forgiveness to occur. Let the shift complete. You will feel it when it does. As your forgiveness is accepted within every aspect of your Being, can you feel the larger sense of your Self, your peace? Can you feel the freedom of forgiveness? This feeling of peace, freedom, and calm is the eye of the storm. This is the center of our attitude, our behavior, our choices, our Being and our knowing.

As you feel the shift complete, say, "*So Be It.*" And, so it is.

Uncovering Your Blueprint

Your Soul continually directs your choices along paths that lead you through necessary experiences that enable you to fulfill your specific purpose during your time on Earth. It is always directing you to pay attention to what is happening in the present moment, and to act upon these inner directives that allow you to navigate your environment with skill, grace and masterful timing. When you listen to your inner guidance above all else and then act on its wisdom, your life can unfold as your Soul designed.

We all have intentions for incarnating, and a Soul-designed plan for achieving these intentions. The Ancient Ones describe this plan as our "blueprint", and each one is unique. Every one of us has a blueprint within us and, it is revealed to us in our heart when we pay close attention. It has been within us since our birth and is always available to us throughout our lives. It is the heart's knowing of our own divine plan that sets us free from the tyranny of the ego-mind and the ego world, so that we can live as expressions of our divine purpose.

Listen carefully as your Soul's voice guides you through the unfolding of your Soul-designed life. It is using your blueprint, designed by your Soul for you—and only you. Once you uncover it, you can follow your own truth over any subconscious program or outside opinion because of your clear sense of purpose and direction.

In time, your confidence in your inner guidance, your individual truth, will become unshakable. You will want to follow your guidance and stand by it with firm determination. However, resist any temptation to claim your truth as the truth for someone else. Your blueprint is not applicable for anyone else's life; it is for yours alone.

Your ongoing goal is to uncover and express your Soul's purpose. To allow this process, you must find calmness, peace and clarity within, without interference or distraction. You can listen deeply to that inner voice we all have within us, and follow its direction. This becomes your focus. In silence, as you still your mind, the guidance comes with grace.

Fulfilling Your Mission

As you uncover your blueprint, you gain awareness about your unique mission in life. There is no mission too small, or too large. You may fulfill a desire to be a parent, to help someone in need, or to complete an agreement made with another before incarnating. You may contribute to a larger shift within your local, national or global community. You may be anonymous in your contribution, or world-famous.

We all have missions to fulfill, as well as a true desire to complete them. As you listen within and follow your inner guidance, you will come to recognize hints, clues and indications of the correctness of your path. Your Soul will alert you to the events it has organized for you so you can fulfill your true purpose. You need only to pay attention to the proper signals! Call it serendipity, happenstance, luck, or answered prayer. When you follow your positive feelings, you will enjoy positive experiences because your higher level of consciousness is bringing you into alignment with your original plans.

While you can miss signposts and opportunities because of inattention, it is never too late to complete many portions of your blueprint. Right now, decide to accomplish as much as possible. Determine to uncover and express your blueprint as completely as you can. This decision will ignite a passion from deep within that will fuel a life of joy and fulfillment.

Key Questions for Uncovering Your Blueprint

When you feel centered in your heart, ask your Self the following question and allow the answer to come into your awareness:

"What do I need to know now to be in the highest opportunity for myself and for all?"

Relax. Take your time. Inner guidance comes in many forms. You may see an image or view a scene as in a movie. You may hear an inner voice or have an inner knowing. You may have a felt sense of well-being. It is different for everyone, and we may each experience more than one way of receiving an answer.

Make note of your inner vision, what you hear inside, how you feel or what ideas come to mind. This is how your answers come. Choose the positive interpretation of your answer. If you are not sure about the meaning of what emerges, you may want to ask more clarifying questions.

As you gain clarity about the answer to your question, you may want to apply your new insights. This moves knowledge into wisdom and virtuous action.

When you are ready, ask within, *"What is my next step?"*

The answer may be a strong sense of completion in the awareness, or a clear call to action. It may be another question. Repeat and continue this process. Become a master asker.

Savor Your Soul

Whether you are quietly exploring your own inner universe or actively engaging with the world around you, relating from the heart keeps you in your personal truth and on purpose. Your Soul responds to what is, and remains true to your purpose. If you stop trying to figure things out with your mind, and instead listen within to your Soul's voice, you will find more clarity and make fewer mistakes. If you slow down the mental/emotional hyperactivity that gets you nowhere and leaves you feeling exhausted, and instead center yourself in the stillness of your heart center, the clarity of your inner guidance will allow you to act with swift decisiveness. This is an energizing process, and you may begin to experience the paradox that the slower you go, the faster you get there.

Remember, your Soul has the answer to any question! You can have clarity about the past, awareness of the present and insight into the future. It is all there inside of you. There is no need to go looking anywhere else. We each have our own answers!

At first it takes effort, determination and diligence to listen to the Soul's direction above external influences. If you have been listening within, you already have had a taste of your Soul's guidance. Let that taste blossom into a true desire. Come to honor your own Soul's direction over the man-made rules and systems that have made so many people ignorant of their own true capacity, profound wisdom and inherent divinity.

When you are in your heart center and make a decision in clarity, peace and Self-empowerment, you overwrite your old programs. This creates a new future that is in alignment with your truth, with your blueprint. You can review any decision, whether it was made recently or in the far past, and change your mind. Making a new choice to overwrite the old one changes everything, because that old choice will no longer be repeated (consciously or unconsciously) in a new situation. What you decide now becomes your future. When you make a decision from your heart's knowing, you create the future your Soul desires.

Remember that ego-mind library of beliefs you've been stocking your whole life? This process is a clearing out of the unwanted programs, and a reorganization of your library. Once you understand what a belief is about, and why you have it, you can decide whether to keep it. You are replacing the books in your library that you no longer need with the ones that you truly desire. You are removing the programs that hinder your progress, limit your clarity, and cover over your truth.

You are preparing the conditions for your true desires to unfold as your Soul designed, and this will open up your passion. Passion is the fuel that propels our direction in life. When you feel driven to accomplish a particular purpose, your life opens to excitement and fulfillment. Each day builds upon the last in a multitude of synchronicities. These, at times, seem miraculous, and the mystery of these coincidences sparks your delight in the exhilarating experience you are creating.

We are all fully capable of listening within and hearing our true voice, so practice listening most of all. Become a master asker. Practice builds trust in your knowing, and that trust leads to right action. Right action leads to passion. Listen within, and create a more positive attitude from your heart space. Love your Self!

Raise your consciousness, forgive yourself, and treasure your own inner guidance.

Apply the Wisdom

Copy the following words and apply them to yourself:

I trust my Soul's direction,
My own truth and divinity.
I allow the answers I need
To rise into my heart's knowing.

Read these words daily, perhaps by posting them conspicuously where you can see them, to be a constant reminder of where to find your answers. Create a space of twenty minutes a day to spend time alone in meditative, inner dialog, preferably in the morning.

Everyone likes a reason to stay in bed longer in the morning, so here you are! Get up 20 minutes earlier than usual if you need to, and before you get out of bed start asking questions within. Remember to hold this dialog in your heart center. Protect this time every day, making note of your inner guidance.

From the Ancient Ones: Inner Authority

An individual's inner authority is their Soul. Each incarnated Soul comes in with his or her own design or "Blueprint". This package of information is held within the fifth chakra, near the thyroid gland of each person. It is designed to awaken in stages from adolescence to maturity. Inherent in all human beings is their purpose or mission to be fulfilled.

A mission can be as simple as having children or as grand as becoming a global leader in creating world peace. The job is designed according to one's desire and ability before entering the Earth plane as a woman or man. Everything has meaning, and nothing is too insignificant.

To fulfill one's unique blueprint is the goal of each person. There will be signposts along the way, feelings of expansion or contraction, serendipity and coincidences. All of these things are brought forth from the unseen spiritual aspect of you, that is, your Soul. Listen within to how you truly feel. Follow your true desires. Decide to make your own inner truth your Pole Star and follow it implicitly.

It is never too late to accomplish many of the facets in your design. Though, much can be missed if one is not paying close attention. Still, begin wherever you are to achieve as much as you can, and this very act will ignite the passion deep within your Being. From passion comes joy and a life well lived.

3
Being Your Self –
Acting on Your Soul's Direction

As you build your relationship with your true best friend, your Soul, you will come to desire its consistent communication. In time, your inner voice becomes clearer than any other. And, once you realize that you have your own accurate answers to every question life presents you, you are fully empowered to conduct your life according to your Soul's design.

Giving focused attention to your Soul's guidance changes you. Instead of acting thoughtlessly, you carefully gauge where your decisions are originating from – your heart or your belly. You make sure that your intentions are pure. You check within to ensure the integrity, accuracy and proper timing of your choices.

By uncovering more details of your blueprint you gain more confidence in your direction. Rather than acting from your old ego- mind programming or outside opinion, your new insights and evolved perspectives give you opportunities to act from your personal wisdom, with greater effectiveness. This builds a strong bond between your Soul's guidance and your ego-mind's willingness to follow through. In bringing your body, ego-mind and Soul into full alignment with your purpose, or blueprint, you experience unity within yourself. True joy and fulfillment naturally results.

Your Divine Nature

Whatever you choose to call it, God, Heavenly Father, Divine Mother, Divinity, Source, Life, Love, Nature, or the Universe… what if you accept that the voice you hear in your heart is that of your own divine nature? Can you accept that this inner guidance is the voice of your Soul?

Jesus the Christ accepted his true nature, as did Gautama Buddha and other renowned spiritual teachers. Each of them lived as an example of what is innate within each one of us. Are you willing to take that level of responsibility for your life?

Jesus knew in advance that many would not be able to accept his message of empowerment and peace, and that he would be killed as a result.[xiii] Still, he acted on the inner voice of his divinity and willingly fulfilled his mission. His choice, while extreme from an ego-mind perspective, makes more sense from the Soul's point of view given the effect his teachings have had on the world. Gautama Buddha was a young, wealthy prince with an easy material life. Confronted with the stark contrast between ease and anguish, he left his kingdom and family to accept his Soul's mission – to find the root of human suffering and then share his discovery with the world.[xiv] He decided to act on his Soul's truth even though the ego world of ego-minds would interpret his choice as idiotic or insane. We know, from the effect of his teachings, that his choice was a positive one from the Soul's perspective.

Most of us do not have these kinds of missions, but if we are to live the life of our Soul Self we will have to make decisions that others, and even our own ego-mind, may judge to be crazy or stupid. Are you willing to be the fool for a while, before the true results of your Soul-directed choices reveal themselves? Are you willing to listen within, act on your Soul's guidance and let go of it having to make sense? If so, many benefits can be experienced.

First, you are building a positive, supportive and loving relationship with your Self. When you are willing to listen, you find that your Soul is magnificent! Truly divine! Your Soul's voice *always* wants your highest good and always tells the truth.

Second, your Soul is wise, and the choices you make by following that wisdom become positive changes in your life. You have greater awareness of the direction your next steps are leading toward and so have more clarity about the likely outcome of your decisions. Because of this, you can be confident that your decisions result in positive experiences, and enjoy them when they manifest.

Third, you are embodying your Soul's blueprint. You are aware of your purpose and your mission, so you can confidently fulfill them. You are wasting no time. Every moment matters. Life becomes sustained joy. Are you willing to be that happy?

Making these shifts in consciousness may require you to make decisions that your ego may be uncomfortable with, may rebel against, or may stubbornly refuse to act upon. You must be strong in your determination to put your Soul in charge. You have to trust your knowing and be confident in your Soul-guided decisions.

At first, this may feel more like faith – being sure of what you hope for and certain of what you do not see. Eventually the faith becomes trust as you see the positive results of your choices. Faith in your Self becomes trust in your Self, and trust becomes confidence until you are living in alignment and balance as your Soul Self. Overcoming the ego's control requires faith and strength of Spirit, as many great teachers have demonstrated throughout human history.

Decide, Align, Act

Like the many successful Soul-guided leaders who came before you, you are capable of unifying your body/ego-mind/Soul and expressing your true nature! A thousand years ago the Sufi poet Abusa'id Abolkhayr wrote that the veil between God and his servant is not in heaven or earth. Rather it is in the illusions of the ego-mind. "Remove these," he wrote, "and thou hast attained unto God."[xv] How do we do this? I have found there to be an easy way and a hard way.

It is likely that we would all prefer to become our Soul Self the easy way. However, sometimes the hard way becomes necessary because of resistance, due to attachment to false beliefs, programming or trauma. The easy way is faster, but both roads will get you there. The sooner we are all living our Soul Self Lives the more enjoyable the human experience will be for everyone.

Soul-Centered Decision Making

Hopefully you have been practicing your inner dialog with your Soul, asking as many refining questions as you need in order to get the clarity that you want. Now, you can introduce this five-step process into your practice:

1. Ask Within, *"What is my next step?"*
2. And, *"What else do I need to know so that I can feel clear about my guidance?"*
3. Bring your ego-mind into agreement with your inner guidance.
4. Decide to act on your guidance.
5. Act and follow through.

Once you are clear on what the next step is, decide to do it! Then, ACT on that decision as soon as possible. This is the easy way. Observe the results. In time, your accuracy will improve, and this builds trust and confidence in your Self. You may be surprised at your wisdom!

After incorporating this five-step process into your life as a regular practice, you will likely notice a number of positive and significant changes, beginning with the recognition that you can consciously evolve your perspective. You will shift from dependence to independence to interdependence. In time, you can enjoy the unfolding of your Being, fully responsible and fulfilled, on the path your Soul originally planned.

Even the Hard Way Will Get You There…Eventually

Making life choices from the Soul's guidance brings joy, pleasure and fulfillment. However, while the easy way can be a simple five-step process, there is also a hard way to raise your perceptions and live as your Soul has designed. In the beginning, you are likely to use the method that I like to call, "What to do when the horse has bucked me off, and I am being dragged through the mud."

You may recognize this is happening when you are:

- Having negative thoughts
- Feeling unwell
- Experiencing confusion, anger, resentment or some other negative feeling (and forgetting that these are indicators that you need to pay attention and change something!)
- Behaving as though life is happening to you
- Forcing, ignoring, denying or avoiding

When your ego-mind is running rampant without you Soul in command, you can make decisions that bring negative consequences. Making choices from the consciousness of victimhood, imbalance, negativity, or distorted ego is likely to bring about situations that you do not truly want, and you will eventually experience the negative consequences of your poor choices.

Perhaps somewhere along the way you rebelled. You recognized that outside authority did not feel right, so you rejected it outright. You may have fought against your family, religion, government, or some other aspect of society. Unfortunately, in your rebelliousness you often create more negative experiences, and even model negative behavior for your children and others.

In contrast, if you choose a positive interpretation of what you perceive to be a negative experience, then you can respond from your Soul rather than react from your ego-mind. If you look carefully, there is always a positive meaning in any experience.

Learn to appreciate that the contrast between what you do not like and what you truly desire can motivate or inspire you to create something positive for the future. You can choose higher.

If you have ever been bucked off a horse, fallen off a bicycle, slipped on a frozen sidewalk or had some other accident or mishap occur in your life, at some point during or after the event you most likely paused to replay it in your mind. Most of us become accomplished askers in these moments. You likely asked questions such as:

- "How hurt am I?"
- "Why did this happen?"
- "What did I miss seeing or sensing?"
- "How did my actions lead to this?"
- "How can I learn from this experience?"
- "How can I avoid this in the future?"
- "What do I need in order to heal?"

You probably changed your behavior after the event. Perhaps you got back on the horse or bicycle and paid closer attention to remaining in your seat. Perhaps you put salt on the sidewalk, shoveled off the ice and snow, or walked more carefully the next time. If you were hurt, you probably attended to your injury or sought assistance from someone with the skills to help. Experiences like these teach us to pay attention!

If you were willing to pay thoughtful attention to a physical mishap, then are you not also capable of paying similar attention to mental and emotional issues that would benefit from your focused analysis? You can retrain yourself to see these thoughts, feelings and experiences as opportunities to make positive changes. You can interrupt your destructive thoughts, catch them as they occur and lift them into higher states.

You can choose to see your illness, victimhood thinking or negative feelings as opportunities to pay attention and make a change. Question everything! All aspects of your life can be seen differently from a higher perspective, including your relationships, career, spiritual beliefs, and the activities that occupy your time and attention.

The process of making an improper decision from your ego-mind, experiencing the negative consequences, raising your awareness to see the error of your choice, then making a new one guided by your Soul is the hard way to bring your body/ego-mind/Soul into alignment and balance. It can be painful and it takes time. However, it works! If you wish to move from an ego-driven life to a Soul guided one, I recommend the easier five-step process. Yet, either way will get you there. All rivers lead to the sea, eventually.

The Garden of Your Life

It is helpful to remember that when you make the shift from an ego-driven life to one guided from your Soul there are both internal and external effects. At first, as you begin to apply the wisdom that emerges from your inner dialog, you will experience profound inner changes. The way you see yourself (and treat yourself) will improve. Your self-respect and self-confidence will grow. And, these positive attitudes and feelings will bring about inner experiences of great joy.

Empowered by your positive inner changes, you can look at your past choices differently. You can evaluate your present circumstances from a higher perspective, and naturally desire to make improvements. Then, you can act with wisdom.

If you find that your present circumstances are not what you desire, make new choices. From your higher perspective, some of the new choices you make may be radically different from your old ones. This is progress! Be aware that as you begin to make it known that your clearer insight has led you to change your mind, the echoes of your old choices may grow louder, perhaps even becoming thunderous! The storm may grow stronger as the people in your life react to your new direction. Even though you know that these choices are for your highest good, it may be difficult for others to accept that the changes you are making are *for* you and not *against* them.

In your Soul center, inside the eye of the storm, you can perceive that most people have ego-mind reactions, while few offer true Soul responses. It takes courage to stand by your Soul's guidance in the face of opposition. The ego-mind often has great difficulty with change. It prefers to hold on to the past, the way it was. But, as Nature demonstrates, change and adaptation is constant in life – and necessary. This is the way of the Soul.

While some of your new decisions will have immediate and obvious effects, others may take time to become visible. New choices are like newly planted seeds in a garden. You must be patient, and remain in integrity with your Self to cultivate and protect them as they take root and grow.

Trust your Soul, and through any storm you can remain calm, clear and steady in the confidence of your inner knowing, in the protection of your Self-love. Because of this, you will be empowered to relate to any feedback in a calm manner, and respond with affirmative confidence.

Remember that some of the present experiences that you are having are not necessarily being created currently, but are merely the diminishing effects of your past. Many previous choices may still be having an effect. They may echo forward through your life, like ripples in a pond, until their repercussions are complete.

Over time, you will notice the echoes of past choices taper off. The life that you had previously created will dissolve and resolve. Previous mistakes will become compost for the abundant life you are growing, and the positive fruits of your new decisions will become ripe and delicious.

Utilize Ancient Wisdom Today

Some people reject religion and also abandon much of the useful wisdom teachings found therein. However, even if you do not consider yourself a Christian you could still appreciate that the Bible has many stories of people who asked within and followed divine guidance. For example, Noah built an ark in preparation for a cataclysm unacknowledged by those around him. Moses had the courage to lead the people of Israel out of Egypt against enormous odds, and Jesus prayed in silence and received direct answers. These people listened to a higher Source, a Divine Presence. They listened and received their answers from within.

You can choose to include any source, any system and any philosophy that you want to explore for your own growth and development. The key is to release the fetters of custom and tradition, and bring all wisdom into the current moment. Remember, Spirit is alive and flowing through every heart. However, knowledge is dead information unless it is brought to life through its proper application in our current lives. Lao-tzu summed this up well when he said:

> "When the Tao is lost, there is goodness. When goodness is lost, there is morality. When morality is lost there is ritual. Ritual is the husk of true faith, the beginning of chaos."[xvi]

If you feel guided to read the Bible, the Tao Te Ching, the teachings of Buddha or perhaps the writings of a more recent teacher, you can! You can listen within for the kernel of wisdom within a book, movie or lecture. You can ask, "What wisdom is here that I can accept into my life?" and "How do I apply that wisdom now?" Choose to learn from ancient wisdom by making it current as expressed through your life. Free yourself from the dusty rituals of religion and breathe life into the insights of great teachers by expressing them through your own thoughts, words and deeds.

Conscious Evolution

All life innately desires to adapt and evolve, and as human beings we can consciously do so. When you uncover your purpose and unleash your passion you naturally make new choices to bring your external experiences into alignment with your inner wisdom. It is natural that your higher perspectives will bring about new choices, and they will have great effect on your life.

You have full authority to follow your inner divinity and take responsibility for your choices. As you mature along the spiritual path you move through stages of consciousness. You have a choice to let life be something that happens *to* you, *because* of you, *through* you or *as* you – depending on your perspective and level of Self- responsibility.[xvii]

For example, if you think that life is happening *to* you, then you are choosing the life of the victim, giving authority to something that is outside of yourself. You are showing that your ego-mind is dependent upon something other than your Soul. You must recognize that this is a choice.

Have hope if you think life is happening *to* you. This simply requires a change in attitude. This is powerful, because changing your attitude is about changing your mind. Most of us change our minds all the time! If you do this as a consciousness-raising exercise, you can receive substantial benefit.

Breaking the Chains of Victimhood

You may be like the elephant, raised in captivity with a chain around its ankle, thinking that because it could not break the chain when it was a baby it still could not as a mighty adult. A shift in awareness is all that is needed for it to realize that it could test the chain, break it, and find its freedom.

Breaking the chains of your victim consciousness requires a healthy mental attitude. Think of positive aspects of your life and magnify them! Be grateful for these positive things happening in your life. These are your blessings, count them!

When you count your blessings, your attitude can shift, your mood can lift and your perspective on life becomes more positive and life-affirming. Your inner strength is revealed. Recognizing that life is abundantly full of blessings is an essential shift to gain a higher perspective.

Often, a first step in raising your consciousness is to simply stop doing what hasn't been working. Utilize your feelings as an indicator. Notice what doesn't feel good. Perhaps it's a destructive habit, or a disempowering relationship. Maybe it's the negative beliefs you have adopted or acquired that limit your sense of freedom. You can replace negative behavior with something that does work. Allow your Soul to guide you to what that is!

Perhaps you have blamed another for giving you poor advice, teaching you incorrectly, or acting out of integrity. While it may be useful to listen to the opinions of others, it is up to you to determine their value. You can listen carefully for any truth within outside opinions that may be of benefit to you, and you can follow your own inner guidance.

When you listen to others and speak from your heart, you can communicate authentically. You can notice when others are talking to you from their bellies, and have compassion for their ignorance. You can enjoy a greater awareness that life is more pleasant when lived from you heart, and so choose to relate heart to heart, Soul to Soul, life to life.

Forgiveness is another powerful consciousness raiser. When you stop judging, condemning and appeasing egos, you can bring great relief to your life. Removing judgment prepares the soil for the blessings of love, joy and fulfillment.

Through the process of forgiveness, you come to have more compassion for yourself and others. You gain deeper appreciation for life's challenges, and the opportunities that they present for you to grow and evolve. By choosing the positive interpretation of any situation, you benefit from both your successes and mistakes. This frees you from self-condemnation, and allows you to relax and enjoy life with more passion.

The Pendulum Swing

After you raise yourself up out of victim consciousness, the next stage may be a pendulum swing in the other direction. You may swing from giving your power away to wielding power over others. You may incorrectly allow your ego-mind to take charge. When your ego is pushing for what it wants, you will likely see life as happening *because* of you. The key is to find balance, to give leadership to your Soul (which is aware of the highest good for all) and utilize the skills of your ego-mind to ensure that you are no longer allowing a victim mentality.

Your ego-mind is the source of your will, and while you can will yourself to overcome many challenges, your Soul can open doors that your willpower might never budge. So, although you may push to assert your will, you still may not get the results that you want. Or, you may create situations that you are happy with, yet not have the capacity to maintain them because your underlying negative beliefs sabotage your improved circumstances.

You may think you need recognition and outside rewards to feel motivated to continue your positive actions. You may feel discouraged if you don't get what you want when you want it, and the way you want it. You may feel frustrated at not being able to maintain the positive changes you make. And, at best, the results of your efforts are likely to be mixed when you are acting from a combination of positive Soul guidance and negative ego drive.

Giving your Soul authority in your decisions prepares a solid foundation for everything you build in your life. Deciding to act upon your inner knowing brings your ego-mind into alignment with your Soul, which opens the way for real, positive transformation. When you consult your Soul and act upon its guidance you can overwrite your false beliefs, create the life you desire and sustain it.

Inner Balance

When you are listening within, trusting your inner guidance, and acting on its direction, yet you are still not fully accepting that the knowing comes from *you*, then life is felt as happening *through* you. This is more positive, and much beauty can come from this. In this perspective, you are living from your heart and the higher energies of your Being. Life flows through you and you enjoy the many positive benefits of following your inner knowing.

This is a wonderful state of living because you can accept divinity as expressing through you. At this level of consciousness, you can feel your worthiness to be human, to experience life, and to be an emissary of love, light, peace and abundance. You may still give credit for all this beauty to something outside of you, yet you are experiencing a level of tranquility of mind and trust in life. However, you can experience a sense of fulfillment and joy even greater than this.

When you accept your own divinity, trust your inner knowing, and act upon your clarity of purpose, then you can shift into being your Soul Self. This is when you realize that the voice you have been listening to all along is a higher aspect of you. You have your own answers to life's questions, and you create your own reality. You recognize that it is simple to act on your Soul's direction because that is how you were originally designed to function.

At this level of consciousness, you have dissolved the perceived veil between "God and his servant." This is that state of harmony when the horse and rider are One. The body, ego-mind and Soul are in alignment and agreement, and life is truly joyful and divine.

Know When to Ask for Help

Sometimes in the process of asking within for your answers you bump into turmoil. Often, as you ask further refining questions, you can shift your perspective and the negative experience can transmute into a higher awareness with greater understanding. Yet, at times it may be wise to have help in clearing trauma.

With skilled help, it may be possible to gain a clearer reflection of your Soul's awareness, so that you can open into a higher perspective and shift into positive interpretation. You can receive confirmation of your shift and support in your knowing. This can be immensely helpful in building trust and confidence in your own capabilities.

Follow your inner guidance to find the proper assistance you need. Ask within to be shown where to look and who may assist you. It is vital to practice due diligence to ensure that your guide has reached a level of self-awareness to be of true service to you. Often, with the help of another, you can do more than would be possible on your own.

Once you remove the interfering blocks, life flows more freely and fully, and your new strength supports your continuing expansion into your Soul Self life. You can act on your inner knowing and build faith, trust and confidence in your Self. This strength will be of immense help in mastering your ego and experiencing true oneness within.

Apply the Wisdom

Extend your 20-minute morning meditation practice into active decision-making, then accomplishment. Ask within to be shown how you can implement your inner guidance into physical action. Write down the insights you receive. Use your notes to help you follow through.

Have the courage to act upon your knowing, even if your guidance doesn't make sense at first. Over time, refer back to your notes and compare how things work out. You will likely notice that as you improve your p, your insights will be more accurate and your results positive. Continue to build your skills as a master asker. This is the easy path to fulfilling your blueprint.

From the Ancient Ones: Action

Acting on one's inner guidance builds strength between the Soul's directive and the Ego-mind's willingness to follow through. Together, in union, these aspects form a bond of unity within oneself. In bringing the body/ego-mind/Soul in full alignment with one's purpose, or blueprint, true joy and fulfillment are the result.

Jesus the Christ said, "The Father and I are one", and, "I do the will of him that sent me." These passages can be understood as Jesus (the human personality ego-mind within the body framework) is being guided or directed by his spiritual nature, or Soul, as the father in heaven whose blueprint forms Jesus' purpose or mission.

When you take away the fear of breaking with religious tradition, you can honestly think these words through to an entirely functional conclusion that will bring more meaning to Jesus' other words, "You will do works greater than this".

Do not be afraid to ponder for yourself anything written by another. Utilize your own inner wisdom and ask for personal guidance from your Soul's knowing. You will be amazed at how much wisdom and joy comes forth through this development of inner dialog between the ego-mind and Soul.

All answers to your questions are within you. Seek them from within, and find out for yourself firsthand just how accurate they are. Only you can think for yourself, if you dare to do so. Life is much more satisfying when you are in command of your choices. Take the necessary steps to develop a deep relationship with yourself. Jesus showed the way. He did not heed the false teachings, or warnings of the religious customs of his day. He took a stand for truth, his truth. You can too.

Afterword

Thank you for purchasing and reading this book. In the course of writing a much larger work, *Soul Self Living*, I recognized that the first few chapters of that book had become a complete work unto itself. *Soul Self* is the foundation of *Soul Self Living*. I am delighted to share this book with you, and yes, there is more to come!

Channeled Vibrational Healing Intensives

Whether you are facing a physical illness or injury, suffering from emotional trauma, seeking mental clarity, or desiring energetic or spiritual support for your well-being, you don't need to struggle on your own any more.

Stacey Stephens offers an energy healing service called a Channeled Vibrational Healing Intensive in which The Ancient Ones work through her to perform healings.

Other Offerings to Enrich Your Life at Soul Self Living

Our purpose is to assist humanity to awaken their deep inner knowing from within their Souls, allowing perceptual changes to broaden their acceptance of individual creativity and value, combining with the collective consciousness of the whole to bring about cooperation, harmony and unity for the highest opportunity of all.

It is our desire to be of service in providing this transformative material. We have designed the Soul Self Living website and our books to assist individuals to awaken at their own pace, as their inner process unfolds. We are honored to share in this sacred connection of Souls awakening to their true divinity. May we all come to live a Soul Self life, accepting each individual as a brother or sister, working in unity to bring forth peace, wisdom and love.

We are also honored to deliver the illuminating messages channeled through Stacey by "The Ancient Ones". Their wisdom and guidance is a blessing for all of humanity. We hope their message spreads far and wide.

~ Jack and Stacey Stephens

Find all of the following offerings at SoulSelfLiving.com

Online Course –Awaken Your Soul

In this self-paced online course you can learn how to create more balance, harmony, and well-being in your life. Well-being encompasses every area of your life: physical, emotional, mental, spiritual, energetic, relational, financial, environmental, etc.

The Ancient wisdom made current in this course can help you shift into deeper intimacy with your Soul. As you become best friends with this Divine aspect of yourself, you can improve your own well-being and better assist those you love.

Awaken Your Soul is the complete collection of over 400 messages/lessons from The Ancient Ones channeled over the course of ten years by Stacey Stephens.

Further Reading

The *Messages from The Ancient Ones* Series

If you enjoyed *Soul Self*, you'll also enjoy the 8-part book series, *Messages from The Ancient Ones*.

These books, channeled through Stacey Stephens, contain Universal wisdom for the transformation of individual and collective consciousness. We are so pleased to share them with you now, in this published collection of public communications from The Ancient Ones. Simple, yet profound, each message touches the hearts and Souls of every reader willing to experience more of their divine nature. They are Amazon.com Top 10 Bestsellers.

Express As YOU: Celebrate Your Uniqueness

"This book is a very personal one, in that I wrote it for myself, for my own evolutionary process. It is quite dense, which is why it is not very long, because this is how the Teacher in me teaches myself. I could unpack each paragraph to fill numerous pages, making it a larger book, but I do not wish to think for you. Rather, I desire for you to think for yourself; to learn to rely on your Soul to work with your psyche to unfold from within it what is right for you at the time. This way the book can be reread, each time gaining new insights from within; similar to the way some Master Teachers teach in parables or poems." ~ Stacey Stephens

Find all of the above offerings at SoulSelfLiving.com

References

[i] Lipton, Bruce (2005). *The Biology of Belief.* Carlsbad, CA: Hay House, Inc.

[ii] Brannaman, Buck & Reynolds, William (2004). *Believe: A Horseman's Journey.* Guilford, CT: Lyons Press

[iii] http://naturalhorserider.com/Horsemanship.html. Retrieved 22 April 2012

[iv] Millan, Cesar & Peltier, Melissa (2006). *Cesar's Way: The Natural, Everyday Guide to Understanding and Correcting Common Dog Problems.* New York, NY: Harmony Books

[v] Center for Nonviolent Communication. (2005). *Feelings Inventory.* Retrieved 27 January 2011 from http://www.cnvc.org/Training/feelings-inventory

[vi] McTaggart, Lynne (2007). *The Intention Experiment: Using Your Thoughts to Change Your Life and the World.* New York, NY: Free Press

[vii] Taylor, Eldon (2011). *What If?: The Challenge of Self- Realization.* Carlsbad, CA: Hay House, Inc.

[viii] John 8:32

[ix] Center for Nonviolent Communication. (2005). *Feelings Inventory.* Retrieved 27 January 2011 from http://www.cnvc.org/Training/feelings-inventory

[x] Davidson, Richard (2008, February). *The Heart-Brain Connection: The Neuroscience of Social, Emotional, and Academic Learning* [video file]. Retrieved 30 December 2010 from http://www.edutopia.org/richard-davidson-sel-brain- video

[xi] Teilhard de Chardin, Pierre (1955). *Le Phénomene Humain*. Paris: Éditions du Seuil.

[xii] Weidner, Jay (Producer & Director). (2009). *Infinity: The Ultimate Trip* [Motion Picture]. United States: Sacred Mysteries Productions.

[xiii] Matthew 26:39

[xiv] Chödzin, Sherab (1994). *A Life of the Buddha*. Boston, MA: Shambhala Publications, Inc.

[xv] Browne, Edward (1906). *A Literary History of Persia*. New York, NY: Charles Scribner's Sons.

[xvi] Lao-tzu (1988). *Tao Te Ching: A New English Version*. (Stephen Mitchell, Trans.). New York, NY: Harper Perennial Modern Classics.

[xvii] Beckwith, Michael (2008). *The Life Visioning Process* [Audio Recording]. Louisville, CO: Sounds True, Inc.

About the Author

Jack Stephens is Co-Founder and CEO of Soul Self Living, Inc. He is a permaculture designer with decades of experience in the sustainability movement as an organic gardener, entrepreneur, natural builder, teacher, and organizer. An avid explorer of spiritual philosophies and wisdom traditions, his quest for spiritual fulfillment led him to the door of his Soulmate, now wife, the healing channel for The Ancient Ones, Stacey Stephens. Jack and Stacey founded Soul Self Living to bring forward their vision of a healthy and regenerative human culture that supports and integrates with all of life.

About Soul Self Living

Jack and Stacey Stephens founded Soul Self Living with the intention to assist people to Awaken to the divine power within them, so they may co-create the life that fulfills their Soul's purpose for incarnating here on Earth. To learn more, please visit SoulSelfLiving.com.

www.ingramcontent.com/pod-product-compliance
Lightning Source LLC
LaVergne TN
LVHW051849080426
835512LV00018B/3153